Y.E.S.

50 Years of Community Building

Y.E.S.

50 Years of Community Building

Humboldt State University Press

Humboldt State University Press
Humboldt State University Library
1 Harpst Street
Arcata, California 95521-8299
hsupress@humboldt.edu
digitalcommons.humboldt.edu/hsu_press

©2018 Humboldt State University

This book is licensed under a Creative Commons Attribution-NonCommercial-NoDerivatives 4.0 International License.

Historic images and documents for this book were provided by Humboldt State University Library Special Collections and the Y.E.S. Archives. Images may not be reproduced or transmitted in any form or manner without written permission from the copyright holder.

Use of the book beyond what is permissible through the Creative Commons license requires the written permission of a Humboldt State University Press representative. Please contact Humboldt State University Press for more information.

Content compiled and organized by Amanda Ramirez-Sebree
Body content written by Erika Andrews
Cover and interior design by Sarah Godlin

Y.E.S. - 50 Years of Community Building
Arcata, California: Humboldt State University Press
ISBN-13: 978-1-947112-094

Table of Contents

ix..Foreword
xii...Timeline
1..Introduction
6...1960s
22...1970s
40...1980s
62...1990s
80...2000s
102...2010s
118..Beyond
120.......................................Y.E.S. Programs
122.............................Acknowledgements
126..Intern Team

We dedicate this book to the students, community participants, campus and community partners, and loyal supporters who have contributed so much to Y.E.S. over the past 50 years. We celebrate the rich diversity of backgrounds, ideas and lifestyles, and the shared commitment to social justice.

We thank you for your involvement, support, and caring. Here's to the next 50 years of community building!

The mission of Y.E.S. is to support student-initiated, student-led volunteer programs that meet local community needs. By creating a collaborative, inclusive, and safe environment, students are encouraged to become active creators of their own learning through exploring new ideas, developing leadership, connecting deeply with peers and those they serve, and building meaning through reflection.

> The Y.E.S. program students—Student Program Consultants, Student Directors, and Student Volunteers—have not only developed their own leadership and established their own values of service, they have also served as role models for other university students, staff and faculty, and the off-campus community in developing a passion for community care. The Y.E.S. experience has also enhanced, and continues to enhance, the students' academic and social experience at HSU by providing the students with an opportunity to apply concepts and theoretical frameworks to the service work.

-Randi Darnall Burke,
HSU Employed (1977–2018),
Dean of Students (2008–2018)

Foreword

Youth Educational Services (Y.E.S.) is celebrating 50 years of community engagement and student leadership.

I cannot think of a better way to memorialize this event than sharing a collection of some of the many stories that can be told because of this organization. From 1968 through today, every person that has been involved with Y.E.S. has a story to tell, and it is our goal with this book to share some of these experiences.

I was a student at Humboldt State University from the fall of 2014 through the spring of 2018, and I was involved with Youth Educational Services throughout all four years in several capacities. I got involved by volunteering for three programs: Study

Buddies (Tutorial), Environmental Education, and the Juvenile Hall Recreation Program. Having the initial opportunity to volunteer for these programs allowed me to further immerse myself in the communities outside of Humboldt State University, primarily by working with youth from different populations and neighborhoods. We helped with homework, facilitated science activities, taught environmental stewardship and gardening, and were mentors for these bright students. Additionally, I was continually inspired by the commitment and passion my fellow volunteers and Y.E.S. student leaders exhibited during program meetings and services. I held leadership roles by being a Program Director for Study Buddies, Program Consultant, and Y.E.S. Governing Body Co-Chair. In my last year, I had the wonderful privilege of being the 50th Anniversary Outreach Director and Archive Intern to support the collaboration between Y.E.S. and the HSU Library in creating this book.

    In my final semester of college, I spent many hours uncovering just a fraction of the many experiences and events that have occurred during Y.E.S.'s existence. In the Humboldt Room of the Humboldt State University Library Special Collections, there is a collection of Y.E.S. posters, photos, scrapbooks, documents, and more. It was in here, and in Y.E.S.'s own records, that I rediscovered many of the stories shared in this book. In addition to these archives, Stan Smith, Keaundrey Clark, Kyle Morgan, Melea Smith, and I had the opportunity to interview Y.E.S. alumni and community partners with the goal of filling in gaps of history and recording their personal experiences and reflections at Y.E.S.

    From flipping through old photos and interviewing Y.E.S. alumni, to providing context to the images you will see throughout the rest of these pages, creating this book has proven to be an ambitious project. I believe I speak for everyone at Y.E.S. and the HSU Library when I say that we are proud of what we have produced. With such a rich history, from the initiative that John Woolley and others took to establish this organization, to the creation of Y.E.S.'s first program for folks in the LGBTQIA+ community, there is no way we could record every story. We have included highlights that will hopefully resonate with all of you, the many participants, volunteers, student leaders, staff, and friends who have helped create and sustain the legacy of Y.E.S. Thank you for your support throughout the last 50 years.

Y.E.S. has changed my life in so many wonderful ways, and I am eternally grateful for every opportunity, lesson-learned, friendship, and memory. My involvement with Youth Educational Services was the best part of my college experience. It pushed me every day, sustained my excitement to attend Humboldt State University, and allowed me to learn more about myself and my abilities than any of my experiences in the classroom could have. Thank you to the many friends, mentors, volunteers, and participants that I have met at Y.E.S.

– Amanda Ramirez-Sebree
Y.E.S. alumnus, volunteer, leader, & student staff (2014–2018)
Outstanding Student of the Year (2017–2018)

Timeline

1960s

Spring 1967: John Woolley founds Tutorial and Experimental College

Fall 1967: Tutorial begins service in Manila

Fall 1968: Tutorial changes its name to Youth Educational Services

1969: Comstock House secured

At the end of the academic year 1968–69, there were 11 centers operating with about 100 tutors and 100 tutees

1970s

1971: The Manilla Recreation Program begins

Spring of 1972: Y.E.S. establishes a campus recycling program

1973: 5-H program created, which still runs in 2018 as Hand-In-Hand

1974: Health Education Rap Team (HERT) is established, providing information about health in an objective manner.

1974: The Juvenile Hall Recreation Program begins

Spring 1976: A plan is made to demolish the Y.E.S. House to create a parking lot

1978: Y.E.S. House celebrates its 10 year anniversary

Spring 1978: Y.E.S. moves to its new location: House 91, the Hagopian House

1978: CCAT is established

1979: Together-In-Sign program becomes active

1980s

May 1980: New Morning Intercept program created by Dan Ziagos

May 1980: 3 Y.E.S. students named Women and Men of the Year

Fall of 1984: Y.E.S. enters its first Kinetic Sculpture Race and wins "Worst Honorable Mention" (last place)

Fall of 1988: Y.E.S. quilt designed by Marshall Jett. Later assembled and quilted by Katie's Quilters (and some Adopt-A-Grandparent participants)

1980: CCAT renovates Buck House to use as a live-in demonstration house

1982: Together-In-Sign program turned over to community member parents

1983: Family Focus program created

Spring of 1986: Y.E.S. hosts its first Trash-A-Thon (now called Serve-A-Thon)

1986: SAOP (Southeast Asian Outreach Program) created in response to the growing Laotian community

1987: Building on the *Gad Zukes!* cookbook, *A Taste of Humboldt* cookbook is published

1988: Y.E.S. Trash-A-Thon collects four thousand pounds of trash at Mad River and Samoa beaches

April 1989: Y.E.S. celebrates its 20th anniversary

1990s

April 1990: Hand-In-Hand & Friends Together raise money to take 38 kids to Great America in San Jose.

1991: New Games is established

April 1992: Anti-Violence Gathering on the Arcata Plaza

1993: The Homelessness Network (HomieNet) program began

1994: Puentes is established

1995: Alternative Spring Break is established

1996: Golden Years is brought back (formerly Adopt-A-Grandparent)

2000s

2001: Juvenile Hall Recreation Program is brought back

2006: Y.E.S. establishes VOP, a low-commitment volunteer program with varied project sites

2010: Tutorial changes name to Study Buddies

2013: ASB changes name to STEP UPP (Serve Travel Encourage Progress for Underrepresented People in Poverty)

2015: QMAP, Y.E.S.'s first LGBTQIA+ program, is established

2018: Y.E.S. book published on 50th Anniversary

Introduction

When I enter the front door of the Youth Educational Services (Y.E.S. House), I like to take a moment to scan the more than 70 programs whose names wallpaper the top of the living room walls. Each represents a student-initiated, student-led effort from the past 50 years: to assist seniors to live independently, to mentor or tutor young people, to expose youth to alternatives to competitive games, to educate children and community groups about our natural environment, to provide advocacy services for local LGBTQA+ high school students, or to tackle scores of other issues. Some of the programs have lasted but a year or two. Others have endured since the early days. Some have fledged to become independent community non-profits like the Humboldt Open Door Clinic or 4-H Trail (outdoor experiences for youth with physical challenges) or successful campus programs like the Campus Center for Appropriate Technology (CCAT), the Campus Recycling Program (CRP), and the MultiCultural Center (MCC). It is an extraordinary record of continuous contribution.

As former Y.E.S. Executive Director, Joy Hardin, observed in the foreword for *A Taste of Humboldt* (aka, the Y.E.S.

Cookbook), "Education may begin in the classroom, but it does not end there." For half a century, the Y.E.S. program has provided opportunities for Humboldt State University students to apply what they have been learning through books and lectures to address very real community problems. It has been an incredible incubator for the seeds of ideas, a productive outlet for the boundless energy of students, a wonderful laboratory for some of the most powerful learning available at Humboldt State University, and a source of invaluable service to our community. The faces and names have changed with the flow of time, but the essence of Y.E.S. has remained the same.

I agree with writer and social activist Marge Piercy, who said, "The people I love the best, jump into work head first without dallying in the shallows." These are the students of Y.E.S. For my many years of association with Y.E.S., I was continually inspired by the creativity, the energy, and the heart of the students who brought their passion and idealism to these programs. Y.E.S. has, from the very beginning, been a place predicated on the compelling notion of "YES, We Can."

Many of the Y.E.S. alums have gone on to transfer the skills they developed as volunteers, as program directors, and as program advisors to their lives and careers post-Humboldt State. This has extended the influence of Y.E.S. far beyond Humboldt County. Alumni have served on the United States Commission on National and Community Service, started their own non-profits, joined the Peace Corps and Americorps and Teach for America (to name a few), and most bring that ethic of service to their families and communities.

Of course, Y.E.S. would never have thrived without dedicated community partners, tireless faculty and staff, and the financial support of the Associated Students, the University, and the broader community. It is that team that has been critical to the success of Y.E.S. for the past five decades and will continue to be essential for the years to come.

So while we celebrate this golden anniversary, it is also the perfect time for us to recommit not only to the support of Y.E.S. but to the values demonstrated by Y.E.S. in our own daily lives and in the ways that we treat each other.

– Dr. Rees Hughes
Student Affairs (1986–2008)

> Y.E.S. House taught me that wherever I am in the world, I am capable of making an impact - however, Y.E.S. has equally made an impact on my own life. Y.E.S. House ingrained my personal mantra to consistently keep the community I work with, and the big picture, in mind, no matter where I am, and I am eternally thankful for all my days with Y.E.S.

-Marilyn Liu, Y.E.S. ART Program Director and Program Consultant (2013–2016)

Y.E.S.

1960s

The 60s were a pivotal time in the world. With the war in Vietnam and the Civil Rights Movement, a global fight for social and environmental justice through activism defined the spirit of the decade.

In 1967, driven by his own commitment to social justice and community, John Woolley attended a fateful meeting that would serve as a catalyst for the development of Youth Educational Services (Y.E.S.). This meeting, held at San Francisco State University by the California State College Body President's Association (CSCBPA), immersed Woolley in conversations surrounding experimental colleges and tutorial projects being created all around the country.

Inspired, John returned to Humboldt State University and

started the Tutorial program in the spring of 1967. The longest running program at Y.E.S., Tutorial, now known as Study Buddies, provides tutoring resources to local youth. Based on the "radical" idea of youth teaching youth, peer-to-peer education has become a best practice for all programs at Y.E.S.

> **There was a bit of trepidation about going into the community especially during the anti-war period. There was quite a division between let's say pro-war and anti-war factions and communities… We had to make sure that we kept our focus on what we were there for, and we weren't there to proselytize anti-war sentiments, [but] to make sure we could help kids and provide youth tutoring youth. The concept meant that we mostly helped them read and appreciate education.**
>
> -John Woolley, Y.E.S. Co-Founder (1967–1972)

Y.E.S.

Clipping from the *Lumberjack* in 1968.

Invigorated with new ideas, Woolley recruited some of his peers, namely Walt Sheasby, Fred Nave, and John Woods, to spearhead the Tutorial project in Manila, California. When recollecting the start of Tutorial, Woolley said, "We went down to Arcata Elementary school and asked them if we could use the closed school out in Manila to run a Tutorial project. They were really not ready for us but that's what I did in the beginning, and it changed in '68 when I got funding from the campus student body as well as from a national grant. That's where I expanded my role from being an organizer to then being [program] director in the Manila community, because I really loved what was going on out there."

Y.E.S. Program

Youth Education Services is the bud of a new program. We need the strength and interest of the Student Body to make it grow and function. This program offers you the opportunity to work with community organizations and people, to test your patience and skill and to reward yourself with honest effort. Tutorial seminars, counseling and friendship is what we offer the community. If you feel that four hours of work a week can help you, we know it can help others. We need tutors, administrators and coordinators. If you are interested to find out more, come to the General Orientation on Saturday, September 28, at 12 Noon, in Founders Hall. What we can offer has broad limits, what we do depends on your interest.

1960s

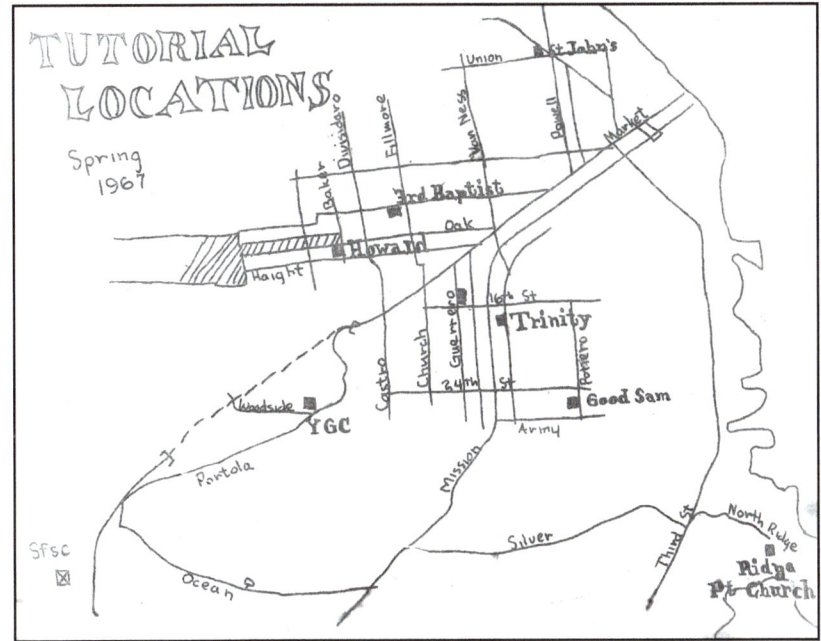

A hand drawn map of the Tutorial locations from Spring 1967

Due to the lack of enrollment and funding, the Manila School located on the Samoa Peninsula (now a community center and Redwood Coast Montessori) had been recently abandoned by the Arcata School District. Samoa, California, was a place of interest for Woolley and the crew because the area had a high concentration of lower income families who, they thought, could benefit from the resources they were planning to provide. Woolley perceived some hesitation from authorities in allowing student activists to use the property, but the collective goal of Woolley and his peers of tutoring children and passion about the project ultimately proved persuasive.

With great tenacity, the crew secured the Manila School and made it ready for their program. The program met twice a week on Tuesdays and Thursdays. Fred Nave was charged with piloting the Tutorial program, which included an initial 10 tutors with their 10 tutees from various locations around Arcata.

The Tutorial program was a great success. By the end of 1967, the project had grown to 70 tutors and an equal amount of "registered" tutees. However, with that volume of participants, Tutorial also experienced problems. Some were

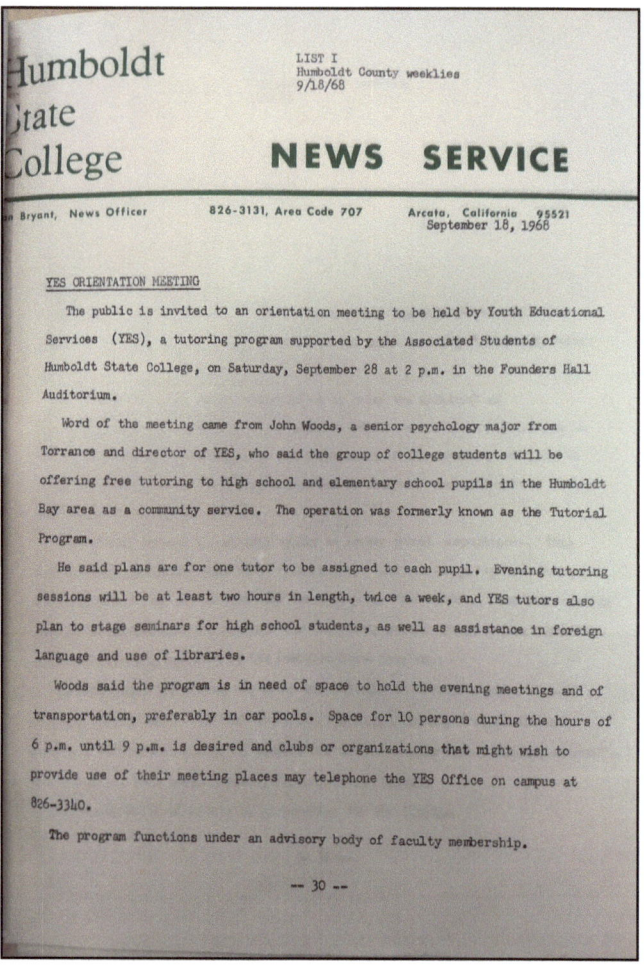

A press release from the early days of Y.E.S.

> "At the closed school there was a jungle gym or park equipment structure. We had just cleared 400 car bodies and all the debris from the mill site and we made a park out of it, but it didn't have any playground equipment. So, in the middle of the night, people went and unleashed it from the old school grounds and took it and put it in the park. Well, that really got people angry at the school district. They said, 'You stole!' We said, 'No, it's still there in Manila, it just happens to be in the park… so there!'"
>
> -John Woolley, Y.E.S. Co-Founder (1967–1972)

Y.E.S.

Humboldt State Campus, 1968.

1960s

Kathryn Corbett, professor in the Social Work department at HSU, was an early supporter of Y.E.S.

simple disciplinary problems, while others, such as vandalism and maintenance, were severe enough to warrant a temporary shut down of Tutorial.

Undiscouraged by the set back, Tutorial was rebranded to become Youth Educational Services, or the easy to remember, the acronym Y.E.S., in Fall of 1968. Y.E.S. was created to provide a structure that would foster the growth of student community projects based on service. The first director of Y.E.S., Ben Fairless, fondly remembers the early days working with John Woolley.

Ben Fairless states "…we were co-conspirators. We both wanted to see a student volunteer agency established, so we started looking around for resources and ideas. [In 1968], Kathryn [Corbett] had assigned me this lower division field work responsibility so I thought that Y.E.S. would be a great vehicle for one of my chief responsibilities to the social work program. It wasn't limited to social work students; it drew interested students from all disciplines. I recognized John [Woolley] as having a lot of leadership qualities, which he capitalized on all of his life. We just kind of bounced ideas back and forth and one thing we realized right off is we needed a permanent place to meet."

> **We did a tremendous amount of camping with the Tutorial kids and the Big Brother/Big Sister kids. We would take them down to Bear Creek south of Rio Dell and camp with them, have bonfires and tell them spooky stories, and that was just a lot of fun.**

-Ben Fairless, Y.E.S. Director (1968-1971) and HSU Professor of Social Work

A snapshot of the campus in 1969.

Kathryn Corbett facilitated the acquisition of Comstock House (House 57 behind the HSU Library) as a new central office for Y.E.S. operations, and with the new stability, Y.E.S. leaders set about expanding the program. John Woods decided the best way to accommodate the growing Tutorial program, which now boasted over 100 tutors and the same amount

A catalog for The Experimental College.

of tutees, would be to meet at one of the 11 centers. The centers were held in church buildings in Arcata, Eureka, Sunny Brae, Bayside, Blue Lake, and McKinleyville, along with two centers located in the private homes of gracious people in Manila. These centers and the community members who facilitated their use all contributed to the growing needs of the evolving project.

The programs that emerged out of these fruitful three years were: Tutorial (elementary level was established in 1968, high school level

The Comstock house was an early home for Y.E.S.

in 1969); Big Brother; Project Small Kids (a program working with preschool-aged children, similar to modern day Head Start); Experimental College - Revamped; Helping Hands (a program geared towards people with disabilities); and Consumer Education Program for residents in Manila.

By the end of the 1960s, 6–8% of the student body of Humboldt State College had volunteered with Y.E.S., which at the time was twice the national average for similar organizations. There were roughly 150 volunteers in Tutorial and 50–150 volunteers in other programs. The Y.E.S staff worked hard, but they also had a lot of fun. In fact, many of the Y.E.S. programs involved camping in the northern California coast and redwoods.

Y.E.S.

While strong volunteerism and activism was a key component in the start and growth of Y.E.S. in the first decade, it was also clear that combining fun with learning made these rewarding experiences and would ensure continued growth and participation in the program into the 1970s.

> **Youth Mentoring Program (YMP) was life-changing for me… to have my little buddy that I was assigned to. I could never have imagined that meeting this six-year-old however many years ago would [5 years later] turn into me going to a birthday dinner with an eleven-year-old and her family. It's really cool the bonds you can make with Y.E.S. It is special in that way. Where you have the ability to really get to know people.**
> - Amanda Near, YMP Volunteer,
> QMAP Co-Founder and Director
> (2013–2016)

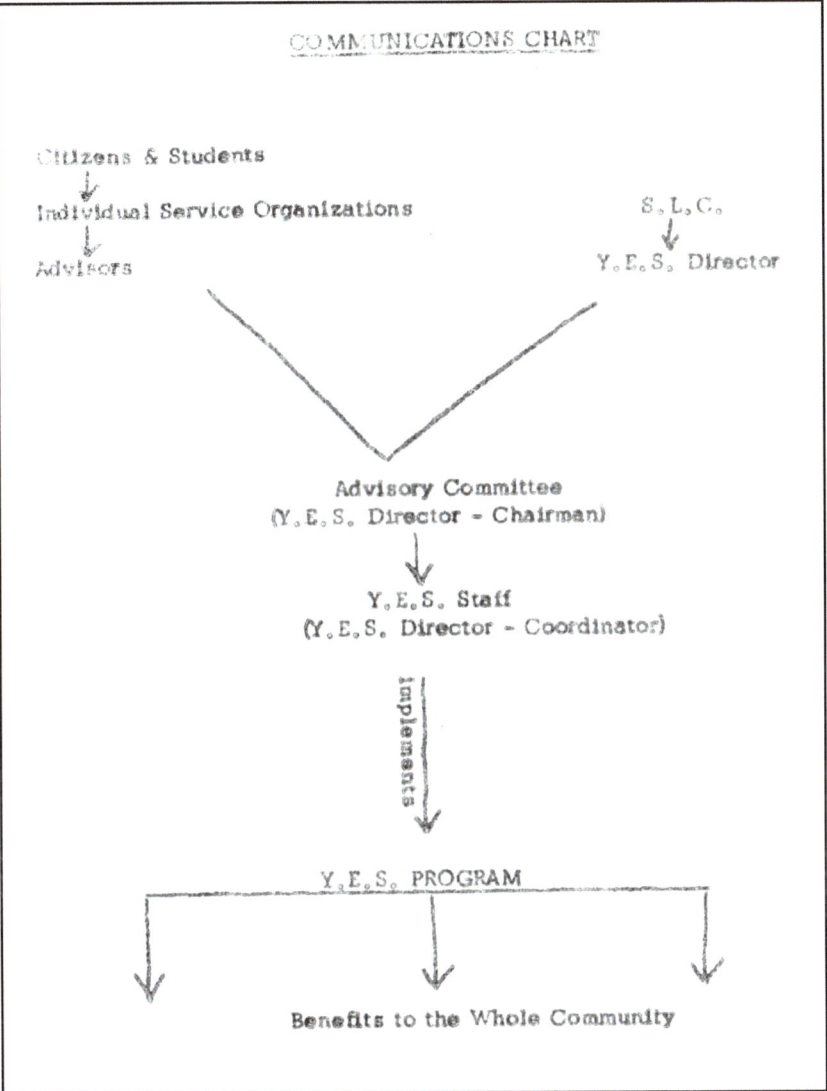

The original communications chart drafted in the 1960s

> **Y.E.S. has this culture, this safe space, where you can fail. You can full on fail at something at Y.E.S. House and it won't be the end of the world. I grew my confidence from Y.E.S. and being able to take more leaps, more chances.**
>
> -Diana Diyarza
> Study Buddies Director, Program Consultant, QMAP Co-Founder and Director (2011–2016)

Y.E.S.

1970s

After Y.E.S. formed in the late 1960s, it quickly emerged into the largest volunteer organization in Humboldt County. In October of 1970, Y.E.S. had ten programs and 300 volunteers. By December of the same year, Y.E.S. added two programs and 100 more volunteers. The 12 Y.E.S. programs included: Elementary Tutorial, High School Tutorial, Project Small Kid, Helping Hands, Big Brother/Sister, Educational Supportive Services, Adult Aid, Consumer Services, Experimental College, Film Forum, Drug Abuse Program, and a research program meant to measure the effects of prolonged informal contact between students and police. With such rapid cultivation came a need for proper funding. Fortunately, Y.E.S. was able to secure a budget increase from $15,000 to $20,000 annually thanks to the Associated Students and other government funds. A United Way campus-wide campaign also began providing support for Y.E.S. programs this decade.

At the beginning of 1971, Ben Fairless passed on his directorship to Ginger Garness, one of the original volunteers of the Tutorial Project from 1967. Elementary Tutorial expanded to nine centers

1970s

Environmental Education volunteers and kids at Wolf Creek Camp.

Y.E.S.

Kids experiment with zucchini during the Nutrition for Kids program implemented in the 1970s.

1970s

Recycling drop-off to open at YES

A recycling drop-off point will open on April 10 in the basement of the Youth Educational Services (YES) House 57.

Drop-offs can be made Monday through Thursday from 8 a.m. to 10 a.m. and from 4 p.m. to 5:30 p.m., and on Fridays from 10 a.m. to 1 p.m. All aluminum cans are to be smashed, paper is to be removed from cans and bottles and papers are to be stacked and tied.

Persons are requested to bring in recyclables only during the hours mentioned.

On Saturdays, YES would appreciate anyone with a pick-up truck coming by the house to help remove the recyclables so the house will not become a fire hazard.

The April 5, 1972 edition of the *Lumberjack* included a blurb about the Campus Recycling Program.

to accommodate the growing project. In efforts to reduce waste on campus, the Campus Recycling Program was established in 1972. In collaboration with Arcata Community Recycling Center, Sudent Legislative Council, and Edward "Buzz" Webb (former HSU Vice President of Student Affairs), this program accepted recyclables during designated hours. The Campus Recycling Program was discontinued in 1980, because recyclables left in the Y.E.S. basement over the summer were creating unsanitary conditions in the house. Fortunately, the legacy of the program didn't end there. Mark Bowers, the Campus Recycling Program director at the time, became the manager of the Arcata Community Recycling Center in 1980.

Other programs started in the 1970s enjoyed greater longevity and continue to flourish today. In 1973, the Adopt-a-Grandparent program (changed to Golden Years in 1996) started to work with seniors to create friendships between generations by matching volunteers in a one-to-one relationship with seniors in the community. Volunteers planned social group activities to enhance the relationships between senior 'grandparents' and their volunteer 'grandchildren.' Volunteers made weekly home visits to assist with gardening and other housekeeping tasks that allowed older adults to maintain their independent living.

The Golden Years program started in the late 1970s as the Adopt-a-Grandparent Program.

> When students provide service to our residents, the quality is amazing. Our residents truly value the Golden Years' willingness to assist them with the daily tasks they can no longer perform. Simple things like dishes, putting up a picture, etc., can be difficult. Not only do the students assist, they bring their enthusiasm and contagious smiles which are valued.
>
> -Kristen Nelson,
> Service Coordinator
> at Eureka Silvercrest Residences

In recent years, Golden Years concluded doing home visits and began volunteering at Silvercrest, an affordable housing option for seniors living in Eureka.

Closely tied to the goals of 4-H (Head, Heart, Hands, Health), 5-H emerged as a program in 1973 and continues today as Hand-In-Hand. Volunteers of this program drew on their own unique skills and experiences to arrange activities such as games, field trips, and environmental activities for underserved children. The hours spent together laughing, growing, and sharing brought personal growth and self-awareness to volunteers and children alike. Today, the program focuses on building relationships with children and youth who have been involved in foster care.

Juvenile Hall Recreation Program (JHRP) ran from approximately 1974 to

This pamphlet is a great example of the art used for many small publications around this time.

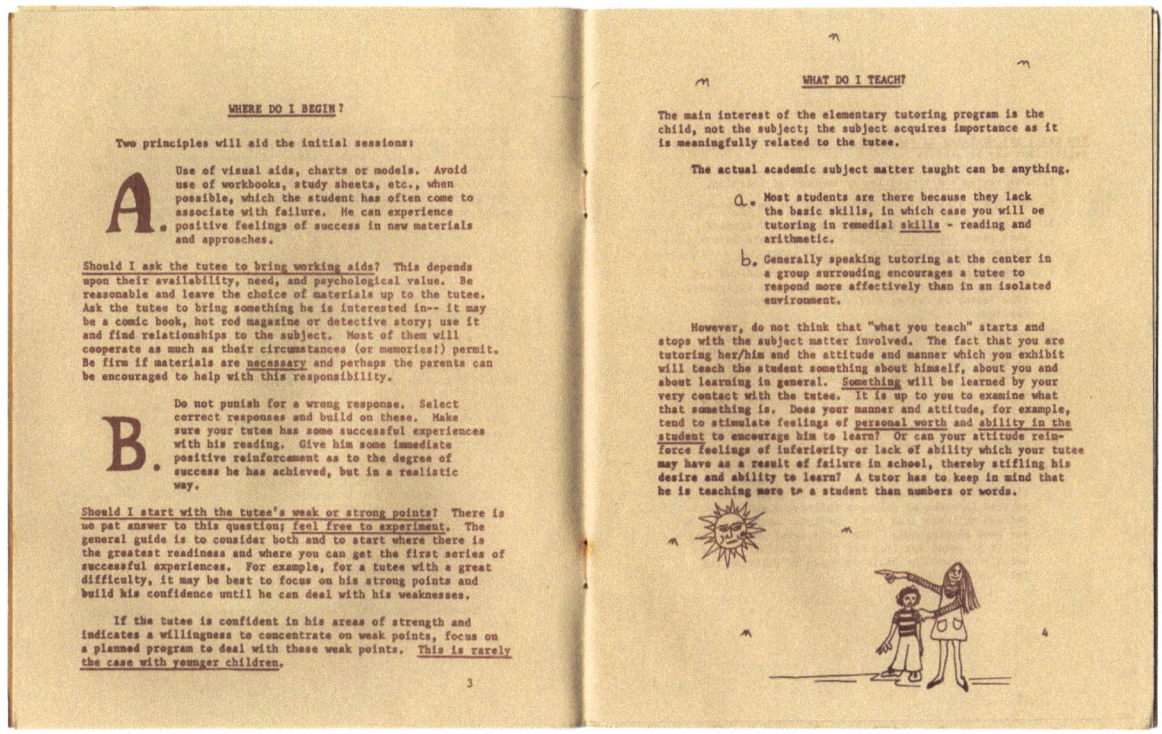

A teaching guide published by Y.E.S. to aid tutors in their instruction.

1980, and only after a few years break, thrives today as one of the most popular and long-standing programs at Y.E.S. The volunteers in the program engage kids in games, sports, dancing, arts, crafts, and other activities they might be interested in. The volunteers provide social connections and productive distractions to youth in difficult situations, helping to build bonds with the kids as mentors and friends.

> **When you see a kid that says 'Hey, I remember you, you came in and worked with me in juvenile hall and said some things to me.' Those are the times that you realize you made a difference to that youth, so keeping that in mind is important. Those are the special moments for me.**

-Ray Watson, Facility Manager, Humboldt County Juvenile Hall

1970s

Educating participants about the environment started in the 1970s.

Environmental Education is another program that has a long-standing history at Y.E.S. Started in 1976, this program worked with elementary school children and community groups to create a greater awareness of the environment. Volunteers provided presentations and workshops on recycling, energy conservation, gardening, and related topics. In 1979, Discovery (later renamed LEAP) was created for people with disabilities and/or limited accessibility. At the time of its establishment, participants in the program were able to join volunteers in experiencing the giant redwoods, ocean waves, the flight of a blue heron, or the excitement of a raft trip down the river – activities that they might not otherwise have had the chance to experience.

In October 1978, the Y.E.S. program moved into the Hagopian House. In the same year, Y.E.S. started a successful program called Cultural Exchange, which established a peer-to-peer buddy system between exchange students and American students.

Many noteworthy programs started in the 1970s did not survive out of the 1980s or 1990s. Nutrition for Kids (1973–1990) volunteers instructed children in nutritional education, food preparation, health, physical fitness, and the joy of choosing nutritious food over junk food.

1970s

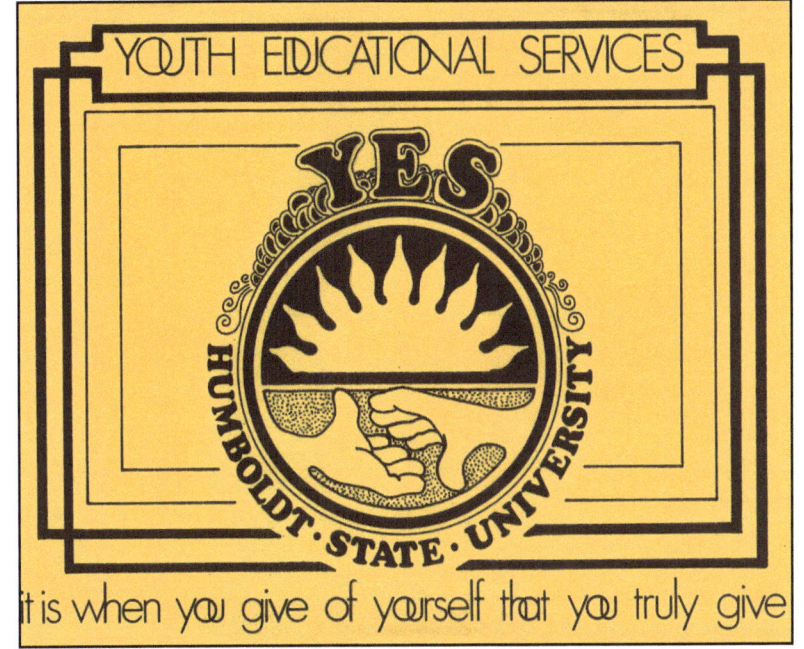

One of the artistic flyers, pamphlets, and publication covers that were created in the 1970s.

Inmates Need Daily Exercise and Education to Develop (INDEED) (1977–1983) gave inmates at the Humboldt County Jail the chance to stay in touch with the outside world through personal interactions and special activities such as sports, craft projects, movies, and presentations. One project, the Inmate Poetry Book, has been preserved and provides moving insights of those behind bars. Horizons Unlimited (1976–1988) partnered volunteers in one-on-one relationships with individuals with developmental disabilities. The friendships

Hand-In-Hand volunteers drew on their own unique skills and experiences to arrange activities such as games, field trips, and environmental activities for underserved children.

made offered growth and learning experiences for both the volunteers and participants alike.

In 1978, Y.E.S. celebrated their 10th anniversary at the recently built Nelson Hall East and West. The anniversary event included juggling, live music, folk dancing, movies, and lots of delicious food. Former 1970s executive directors Ginger Garness and Bruce Siggson, the current executive director Pamela Kambur (1977–1980), and all the volunteers involved in the program certainly had plenty to celebrate. The 1970s were a time of rapid

1970s

> "When you're working with kids who face adversity in their lives, one of the best things for them is to be able to see a familiar face again and again and again, even if it's for a narrow window. Even a small commitment, but one that's reliable, is eons more impactful than anything else. Groups like Hand-In-Hand and Study Buddies [a later iteration of Tutorial] and Environmental Education that make a commitment to come out here each week just do immeasurably beneficial work. The kids in our programs and the community members all know them by name, love them, and are horribly sad when they go on winter and summer break."

-Mark Weller, Deputy Director, Westside Community Improvement Association

Y.E.S.

growth and led to the inception of some of the longest-running programs at Y.E.S. By the end of this decade, Y.E.S. was more than ready for the 1980s and even bigger aspirations for the future.

Gad Zukes! The zucchini recipe booklet published in the 1970s.

Programs that were active during the 10th Anniversary of Y.E.S.

Tutorial, 1968–present
Youth Mentoring Program, 1969–present
Adopt-a-Grandparent, 1973–1990
Nutrition for Kids, 1973–1990
Hand-In-Hand, 1973–present
Health Education Rap Team, 1974–1980
Juvenile Hall Recreation Program, 1974–1980
Legal Information & Referral Service, 1974–1980
Consumer Information Advocate, 1975–1978
MONEY, 1967–1979
Friends, 1976–1983
Connections, 1976–1986
Horizons Unlimited, 1976–1988
Environmental Education, 1976–present
INDEED, 1977–1983
Wertman the Wizard, 1977–1978
Welfare Outreach, 1977–1978
Children's Community Garden Project, 1977–1978
Volunteers in Tax Assistance, 1977–1979
Greenpeace Sea Watch, 1978–1984
Together in Sign, 1978–1980
Cultural Exchange, 1978–1985
YES Travel, 1978–1980
Campus Center for Appropriate Technology, 1978–1981

"
I can honestly say that I don't know who or where I'd be without Y.E.S. It gave me so many skills that my coursework at HSU could never have given me. I am able to talk to large groups with no fear; I can manage a group of my peers, I can organize a schedule, I can reach out to the community with confidence and the list goes on. Without Y.E.S. I wouldn't have an amazing personal and professional network of people who I can count on and who can count on me, for life. Thanks so much to Y.E.S. and to all the people who make it what it is.
"

-Jenn Bradley, Puentes Director
and Program Consultant
(2013–2017)

Y.E.S.

1980s

Y.E.S. volunteers built on the rapid expansion of the 1960s and 1970s to solidify Y.E.S. House's reputation as a place for student leadership and innovation. The 1980s saw Y.E.S. pilot programs that would morph into new programs or even into standalone programs beyond Y.E.S. In May of 1980, former director of the Juvenile Hall Recreation Program (JHRP) Dan Ziagos established a program called New Morning Intercept (NMI), an offshoot of the JHRP and the MENTOR program. NMI secured a $177,000 grant from Bill Gates to provide a treatment program for youth with mental illnesses living in Humboldt County.

In 1981, the Campus Center for Appropriate Technology (CCAT), which started at Y.E.S. in 1978, developed into one of these singular programs supported by the Associated Students. Today, the student-managed, student-funded live-in demonstration home continues to test sustainable operations with low environmental impact technologies.

1980s

Some of the Kinetic Sculpture Crew: Joy Hardin, Phil Finkel, Cyndey Carney, Mae Conroy, and Kim Weir. They received the "Best Costumes" award.

That same year, Y.E.S. student leader Susan Allen founded and directed Kids Club of Manila. In a November 18, 1981 *Lumberjack* interview, Allen explained how she hoped that young people would become active participants in the program and become directly involved in the planning and decision making. Never intended to be a long-standing Y.E.S. program, Allen envisioned that enough students, parents, and community members would get involved to start managing the program and recreational services for themselves. Allen and her fellow student volunteers saw this vision accomplished when they were able to turn the program over to the community in 1982.

Another program that graduated from Y.E.S. was Together-in-Sign. Active in the late 1970s, Together-in-Sign fostered a

> **CCAT**
>
> The Campus Center for Appropriate Technology announces the Grand Opening of its Appropriate Technology demonstration home, The Buck House on May 21. The opening is a culmination of a three year effort on the part of student volunteers to provide the campus and community with an education and research facility regarding the installation and efficiencies of alternative energies and resource recycling. The all-day Saturday event will feature guided tours of the facility, opening ceremonies, and addresses from speakers including President Alistair McCrone and Supervisor Wesley Chesbro. Tours will be held every half-hour beginning at 10am.

A *Lumberjack* story about The Campus Center for Appropriate Technology (CCAT).

1980s

Searching through rocky tide pools with the Environmental Education program.

The Campus Center for Appropriate Technology (CCAT) started in 1978.

community-building relationship much like those in the Big Brother/Big Sister program for children with various hearing impairments. The fourth-year director Lisa Bach negotiated with Humboldt Child Care Council (now called Changing Tides Family Services) to adopt Together-in-Sign as a year-round program, where it became Communication First in 1985.

Another program to increase their services and outreach through community partnering was the Legal Information and Referral Service (LIRS). Founded in 1974, LIRS provided

1980s

free information on legal matters to the campus and the community. The volunteers were trained in basic legal research and attended lectures and field trips to expand upon their legal knowledge. The student leaders counseled individuals in small claims court procedures and researched other legal matters with the assistance of local attorneys. In 1987, under the guidance of director Jo-Ann Magnani, LIRS moved from Hagopian House 91 to the Warren House 53, where it collaborated on services with another HSU-based community assistance program called Consumer Action, improving the services of both to the community.

White water rafting on the Klamath River with the Y.E.S. House LEAP Program, thanks to Jim Ritter, LEAP director (wearing hat).

During the 1980s, many programs under Y.E.S. were flourishing and gaining recognition. Combining Discovery and Project Challenge, lifelong friends Jim Ritter, Bill Halliday, Dave Nakamura, and Jeff Kellog brought their passion for outdoor adventure to create Leadership Education Adventure Program (LEAP) in 1982. LEAP provided low-cost opportunities for youth affected by poverty in order to build trust, self-esteem, leadership, and teamwork skills. LEAP gave volunteers a chance to practice leadership skills. and share their love of the outdoors with the community.

> **Rafting is super fun, and for a young person in our community who would never have the chance to do this otherwise, getting out on the river is very powerful. Adventure challenge provides amazing learning opportunities. It teaches kids teamwork and helps them learn about setting goals and thinking about where they want to go in the world.**

-Jim Ritter, LEAP Director
(1979–1984)

> "I got involved in LEAP during middle school and continued through much of high school. It was always challenging, not just the physical aspects of climbing, boating, and hiking — but also the social interactions that came with leadership and team training. It was also hugely rewarding. I made lasting friendships. I recall cheering those friends as they overcame their fear of heights at a weekend ropes course, and finding courage while they cheered for me. I remember crying tears of joy at the end of that weekend. It was transformative."

-Grant Scott-Goforth,
LEAP Youth Participant (1995–1997)

Northcoast L.E.A.P. forms as programs merge

By Mary Struhs
Y.E.S. Community Outreach Director

It has been said at Y.E.S. that the long-term goal of every Y.E.S. program is to someday "grow up and leave home." For two programs, Project Challenge and Discovery, the time is drawing nearer for their departure from Y.E.S.

Since last spring, the two programs have been developing a plan to merge into one program, entitled Leadership Education Adventure Programs (L.E.A.P.) Northcoast, and move out of Y.E.S. The first phase of their plan, merger, is near completion. L.E.A.P. Northcoast Co-Director Jeff Kellogg remarked that, "Although it's not official, we consider ourselves one program already." The second phase, autonomy, is expected, by Kellogg and his co-director, Dave

Riding the rapids

Discovery has provided whitewater river rafting experiences on the two former Project Challenge and Discovery directors, Bill Halliday, mer, with a total of 158 youths expected to be served during the

Family Focus was founded and co-directed by Marcy Foster and Belle Walter in 1983 to provide resources to adolescent mothers. In an October 1984 *Lumberjack* article, Foster and Walter explained their difficulties being teenage parents and having an "overwhelming sense of powerlessness and a lack of self-confidence." The program paired adult volunteers with teenage mothers to provide support through encouragement, empowerment, and friendship. Walter

Y.E.S.

Y.E.S. partnered with theater groups to fundraise for their many programs

would go on to say the program volunteers use themselves "as agents to find the good things in what the mothers are doing." In 1986, in order to help fund Family Focus, North Coast Repertory Theatre put on a production of "Wait Until Dark," with the proceeds benefiting the program. Foster and Walter received the 1984 Soroptimist International of Arcata Women Helping Women Award for their work with Family Focus. The program continued at Y.E.S. until 2001.

1980s

Students enthusiastically showcase Y.E.S. t-shirts and a new banner.

Southeast Asian Outreach Program (SAOP), later changed to Refugee Extension Program, ran from 1986–2006 to support the growing Laotian community who came to Humboldt County as refugees after the Vietnam War. One of the founders of SAOP, Bob Bouvier, stated in a *Lumberjack* article: "We want to set up a support system to help break down communication and cultural barriers without compromising their own culture." In collaboration with the Peace Corps and the English as a Second Language Program (ESL), the Hmong community members were provided with resources to maintain self-resilience in a new

> **In 1989 I volunteered with 4-H LEAP and later co-directed the summer program. I learned skills and gained confidence which launched my 20 year professional career of leading environmental education/wilderness expeditions for clients and students of all ages. The real-life experiences that connected me with the community were some of the best learning opportunities as a student at HSU.**

-Lora Colten, Y.E.S. Volunteer (1988–1994)

1980s

The Tacky Awards (now called Director Appreciation) was always a colorful event and special time to celebrate student leaders.

home and alleviate the effects of their displacement. By 1988, SAOP worked with 50 families in Humboldt County.

As Y.E.S. became increasingly recognized on campus for its work, so too did its alumni and student leaders. One of the initial founders of Y.E.S., Ben Fairless, became a professor at HSU's Department of Social Work and would serve as a long-time advisor and guiding force for Y.E.S. Three Y.E.S. student leaders would be named Women and Men of the Year (now

Y.E.S.

Phil Finkel and Cyndy Carney pose at the Tacky Awards.

the Outstanding Student Awards): Maureen McGarry, Director of Together (1978–1979) and Connections (1980); Bill DeRecat, Y.E.S. program co-founder and director (1978–1979); and Lynn Boitano, volunteer of the Legal Information and Referral Service (1978) and Campus Recycling Program (1979–1980). Additionally, former director of the Campus Recycling Program, Mark Bowers, went on to become the Manager of the Arcata Community Recycling Center.

1980s

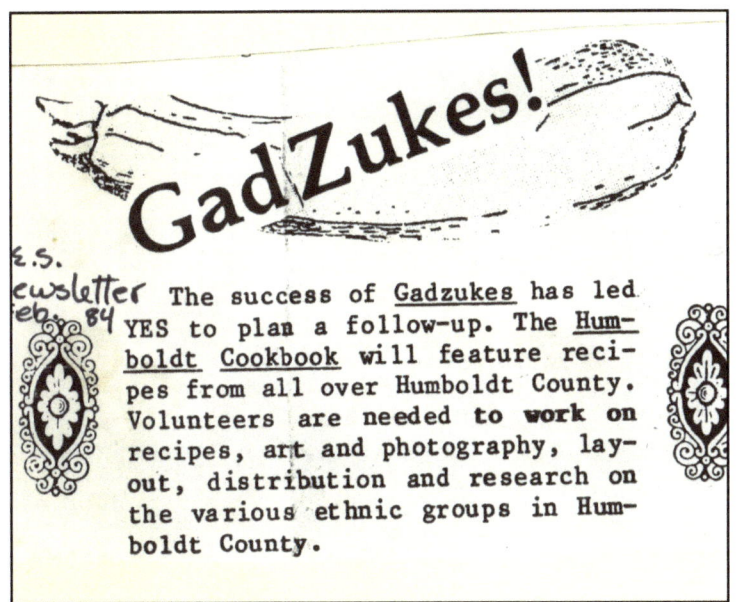

The *Gad Zukes!* cookbook was the predecessor to the more expansive cookbook, *A Taste of Humboldt.*

Leadership development of Y.E.S. students and staff led to the start of Y.E.S.'s own recognition and award events. Dr. Joy Hardin, a former Y.E.S. Executive Director, fashioned the first "Tacky Awards" in 1980. With no money to spare, Hardin and the student leaders pitched in to create a parody award show to honor the directors. Today, the Tacky Awards are known by the more formal name of Director Appreciation, but the same fun and collaborative spirit remains.

Marjorie Fitzpatrick had a dream of creating a cookbook whose proceeds would be used as the source of perpetual funding for scholarships for Y.E.S. program directors. This resulted in the creation of *A Taste of Humboldt* cookbook, based on the zucchini-inspired *Gad Zukes!* cookbook in the 1970s. This fundraising has resulted in the The Marjorie Fitzpatrick

Y.E.S.

> " This cookbook was made financially possible because local people believed in our goal: providing scholarships to those students who spend long hours in direct community service. "

- Marjorie Fitzpatrick, *A Taste of Humboldt* cookbook

1980s

In 1984, the *Gad Zukes!* cookbook inspired Y.E.S. to enter the Humboldt Kinetic Sculpture Race with a namesake stuffed zucchini entry, where it won "Worst Honorable Mention." Here Kim Weir displays the coveted award.

Cookbook Scholarship, which to this day awards approximately $1,500 per semester to very deserving Y.E.S. student directors. The scholarship is administered by the Humboldt Area Foundation who also gave the scholarship fund a $15,000 matching grant that was the basis for raising an equal amount from members of the community. To date, the scholarship has awarded a total of $67,513.81 in scholarships.

The finishing touches are put on the iconic Y.E.S. quilt by members of Katie's Quilters, 1989.

In 1986, Y.E.S. held its first Trash-A-Thon (later to turn into Serve-a-Thon). Started to clean-up the community and raise funds for the various programs under Y.E.S., the first-year volunteers picked up a staggering 800 pounds of trash.

The iconic Y.E.S. Quilt, designed in fall 1988 by Marshall Jett, was assembled and quilted with care by Katie's Quilters. The quilt was even stitched with love by some of the participants of Adopt-a-Grandparent. The Y.E.S. quilt is still proudly displayed at Y.E.S. to this day.

The *Lumberjack* profiled the ideal director, complete with sense of humor and pack full of schoolbooks.

> I wanted to volunteer for a large part of my life. As soon as I walked through the door [of Y.E.S.] I was hooked. I learned how to be a team player, how to collaborate on projects. Communication is one of my strong suits and has only gotten better at Y.E.S. I would say do it 100%! There's no type of person that wouldn't find something at Y.E.S. Y.E.S. has been a life-changing experience and helped me prepare for the life and bright future that I want to pursue. I don't think I would be able to pursue that without what I learned at Y.E.S.

-Alex Banaskiewicz,
Puentes Director
(2017–2018)

Y.E.S.

1990s

In the 1990s, the programs at Y.E.S. continued reaching great feats because of dedicated staff and student volunteers. Y.E.S. also regularly adapted to the times and to the interests of staff and volunteers. Popular programs returned, others were renamed, a few branched off to become independent programs and one became its own department. This decade produced the organizational structure that is currently in place at Y.E.S. In April 1992, Y.E.S. participated in an anti-violence gathering on Arcata Plaza with live music and a rally. Events like this defined the last decade of the millennium, speaking to the ongoing power and legacy of Y.E.S.

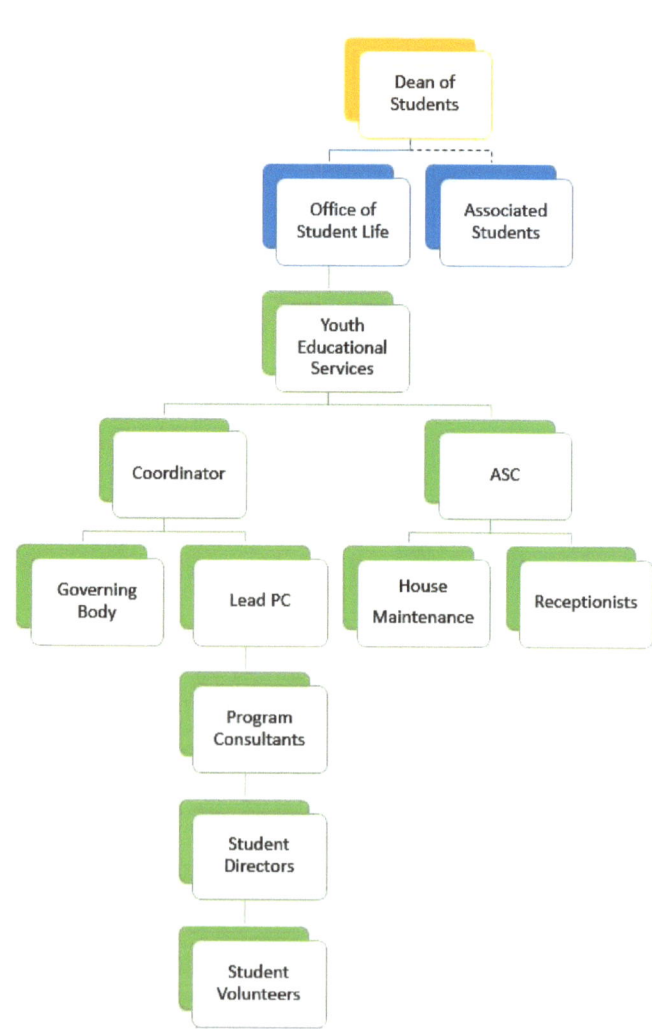

1990s

An anti-violence rally was held in the Arcata Plaza after the Rodney King verdict in 1992.

Y.E.S.

The Y.E.S. staff were the primary organizers of the anti-violence rallies in Arcata's Downtown Plaza.

    A few programs underwent a period of rebranding. Family Focus changed its name to Support Network for Adolescent Parents (SNAP) and SAOP became the Refugee Extension Program (REP). To broaden their community reach, REP strived to educate the community at large about different refugee groups living in Humboldt County. The success of REP led to the development of another program entitled Puentes to serve the Spanish speaking community.

SNAP hosted activities such as horseback rides for adolescent parents.

Established as an independent program in 1994, the program aimed to bridge the cultural gap that exists amongst the Spanish and English speaking communities in Humboldt County.

Adopt-a-Grandparent was re-established in the 1990s under the name Golden Years. The reinvigoration of the program came with new ideas and an expanded mission of service to the elderly community. The program focused on eliminating the isolation and loneliness experienced by the participants of the program, while fostering friendships and long-lasting relationships with the volunteers. It wasn't the only program to remake itself.

Y.E.S.

Refugee Extension Program participants radiate connection and happiness.

Programs at Y.E.S. filled multicultural services in the community and spoke to the need of more integrated services. Out of demands made by students on the Cultural Roundtable, the MultiCultural Center (MCC) was envisioned over the 1992–1993 academic year with support from Y.E.S., as well as Associated Students, Activities Coordinating Board, Center Arts,

The Refugee Extension Program hosted performances and cultural holiday celebrations.

the Clubs & Activities Office, and Student Affairs. Y.E.S. was instrumental in the successful coordinator search and the MCC opened its doors on August 15, 1993.

Some notable programs that became active in the 1990s and are still active today include: New Games, Homelessness Network, and Alternative Spring Break (now known

Y.E.S.

New Games taught cooperative games to elementary school children.

as STEP UPP). New Games, a program to teach communities how to participate in non-violent and non-competitive games, emerged in 1991. This program for adults and children aims to teach participants and volunteers cooperation, team building, self-expression, and encouragement towards positive self-worth and efficacy.

Founded in 1993, the Homelessness Network, or HomieNet, is a Y.E.S. program that aspires for

1990s

HomieNet offered children additional hands on educational experiences.

the empowerment and support of local children and families experiencing homelessness. Promotion of literacy and self-esteem are just two of the specific goals of this program. HomieNet was created to offer assistance and provide children with additional stimulus and educational experiences to foster their interests and creativity. Volunteers actively seek to encourage and improve humanitarian treatment of people experiencing homelessness.

Y.E.S.

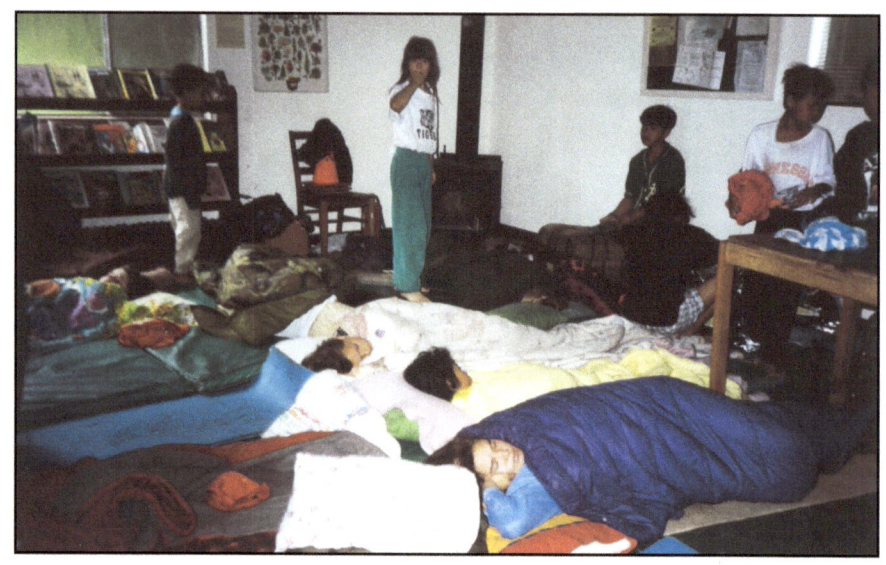

Youth sleepovers were offered as a kids club activity.

> " I was a volunteer for the Y.E.S. House about 22 years ago. Through some personal successes running a program, and many more failures, I learned valuable lessons about organization, time management, and making commitments. That learning experience has been invaluable during my 15 year tenure as the publisher, editor, and owner of *McKinleyville Press*. "
>
> -Jack Durham

1990s

Arts and crafts in the park helped kids explore their creativity in a structured environment.

Another program that addressed homelessness was Alternative Spring Break, a week-long service trip during HSU's Spring Break. Initially developed by Fabrice DeClerck in 1995, the program sent bus loads of students to work with an orphanage in Tijuana, Mexico. After several years the program took a more domestic focus and worked with those experiencing poverty and homelessness. Eventually the name was changed

Y.E.S.

Under the SNAP program, adolescent parents and their children came together for activities.

Annie Bolick-Floss in 2018.

to Service Travel Encourage Progress for Underrepresented People in Poverty (STEP UPP) and Sacramento and San Francisco have been the alternating locations of the service projects.

The 1990s were a time of organizational innovations. In the past, Y.E.S. experimented with different internal processes and delegation of work, service, and influence to see what style of organizational infrastructure worked best. In 1994, Executive Director Annie Bolick-Floss worked with Y.E.S. leaders to implement key programmatic and structural processes that are still the foundation of Y.E.S.

Y.E.S.

The Humboldt State Campus was often the venue for Y.E.S. House get togethers involving community children.

operations today, including the Governing Body, the Pilot Program process, and the Program Proposal process.

The Y.E.S. Governing Body acts as a learning tool for students to have the experience of being on an organizational steering committee while also giving its participants tangible skills and real-life leadership experiences. Students are confirmed by their peers to serve on the Governing Body and their duties include: assessing Y.E.S. pilot programs to assure they fit into the mission of Y.E.S.; discussing risk management and fiscal information of Y.E.S.; managing the Marjorie

Fun at Tutorial's "Spring Fever" event in 1996.

Notice the Y.E.S. quilt in the background of this SNAP event.

Fitzpatrick Cookbook Scholarship program; and establishing guidelines, procedures, long-range planning, and staffing structures for the organization.

During the 1990s, Y.E.S. received support from United Way for 14 of its programs. Y.E.S. also launched an open house for students and other members of the community to come and see all that Y.E.S. House has to offer. The open houses continue to this day.

> "My experiences at Y.E.S. were life-changing. My studies at HSU provided me with the fundamental background that helped me along in my career path. However, it was through Y.E.S. that I had experiences that forever altered who I was as a person. The friendships and interpersonal relations with my fellow volunteers and unequaled mentoring from the likes of Joy Hardin and Carlisle Douglas gave me many and varied real-life experiences that I have reflected on and drawn from many times since I directed LEAP in the early 90s. Humboldt State has something living and powerful in the Y.E.S. organization."

-Scott Rion, LEAP Director (Early 1990s), Recreation Planner, Bureau of Land Management

> "As I find myself preparing to leave I don't know what I'll do without the warm friendly family support-like environment that the Y.E.S. House provides. Everyone here has such true concern for one another and I will truly feel an absence in my heart as I go. But I know my time here has changed me and I will always look back at my experiences with joy in my heart and good wishes for everyone I've met there."
>
> —Jeanette (aka Purple),
> Y.E.S. Volunteer

Y.E.S.

2000s

The beginning of the millennium welcomed the return of Juvenile Hall Recreation Program (JHRP) and three new programs into the Y.E.S. family. JHRP found its way back to Y.E.S. in 2001 after a 21-year hiatus, and is now one of the most sought-after programs that run at Y.E.S. At the time of its reinstatement, part of JHRP's mission was (and continues to be) instilling a sense of trust and respect between youths and college volunteers. Regularly scheduled meetings build this bond by demonstrating that the volunteers do care and will show up for them on a regular basis.

Ray Watson, the Facility Manager at the Humboldt County Juvenile Hall, commented about the purpose of JHRP and the symbiotic relationship between the volunteers and the participants: "A lot of our youth come

2000s

The second floor of the Y.E.S. House has been the nerve center for many programs.

from situations where schooling may be the last thing on their mind. We want to expose them to young adults who are living out their dream by going to college and trying to get an education. [The volunteers] try to show them that they can achieve their goals of going to college and getting a college education."

> I think that Y.E.S. helped shape my passion for helping others and my ability to learn empathy. I was able to relate to people I never had the opportunity to meet until I joined Y.E.S. My paradigm was shifted and I grew to be more open to others and opportunities that came my way that I wouldn't have had otherwise. I was able to learn leadership skills that have helped me be successful in my current career. I love Y.E.S. Thanks so much for letting me find myself!

-Concepcion Orozco, JHRP Co-Director and Program Consultant

2000s

Team building exercises build trust and friendship.

Another program that became active in the 2000s was North Coast Music Mentors (NCMM), which provided youth access to private music lessons. With the high cost of one-on-one sessions for aspiring musicians, NCMM volunteers saw an opportunity to teach youth the discipline of musicianship, a skill that goes beyond the ability to play an instrument. By

Homework help is still part of the Tutorial Program in the form of "Study Buddies".

providing children a space to explore their creativity, mentors helped build the students' self-confidence and musical skill, while improving their own teaching experience and communication skills.

In 2006, Y.E.S. volunteers founded the Volunteer Opportunity Program (VOP) and Art, Recreation, Theater (ART). VOP was created for HSU students who aspired to become active volunteers, but could not commit for a semester-long

Participants of one of the many Cultural Exchange events.

volunteer program. VOP facilitated this kind of volunteerism through monthly events such as beach clean ups, removing invasive plant species from land trusts, gardening at local community gardens, walking dogs at local animal shelters, site beautification at community resource centers, and other projects.

Y.E.S.

The ART program provides youth in the community the opportunity to explore art and their creativity. Bridging the gap between logical and creative-based teaching, ART provides children an outlet for self expression through various mediums, including, but not limited to, visual art, theater, and music. ART volunteers engage youth in wonderfully imaginative play and projects, allowing room for their ideas and contributions.

Safety first for these LEAP participants

LEAP facilitates a plethora of outdoor activities, like rock climbing.

The organizational development at Y.E.S. continued through this decade. Fernando Paz explains that the structure of Y.E.S. helped him develop and refine his organizational skills. "[It] helped me understand how to plan, execute, and then reflect." The reflection process, also referred to as the Experiential Learning Cycle, is a key community engagement and service learning practice.

A game of musical chairs at the student director's retreat.

The importance of the reflection cycle was echoed by Lorena Boswell, the Program Manager and Coordinator at Y.E.S. from 2008 to 2016. At a student director retreat, Boswell recalls directors switching from the traditional model of musical chairs to a more cooperative version in which the participants would sit on top of each other instead of getting eliminated after the music stopped. She recalled the student dialogue after this retreat activity. "The

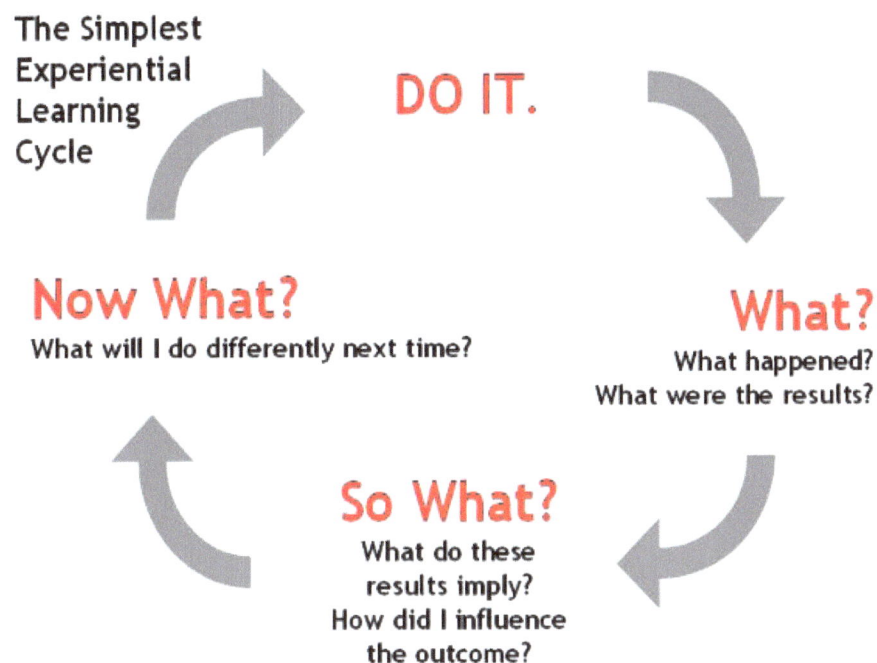

Compiled by Andrea Corney
edbatista.com/2007/10/experietial.html

Reflection Cycle was a handy tool for conversations like this one. It begins with an experience and asks "What?" "So What?" "Now What?" then leading back around to a new experience. Y.E.S. used it all the time, and our musical chairs two-ways activity was no exception. We used

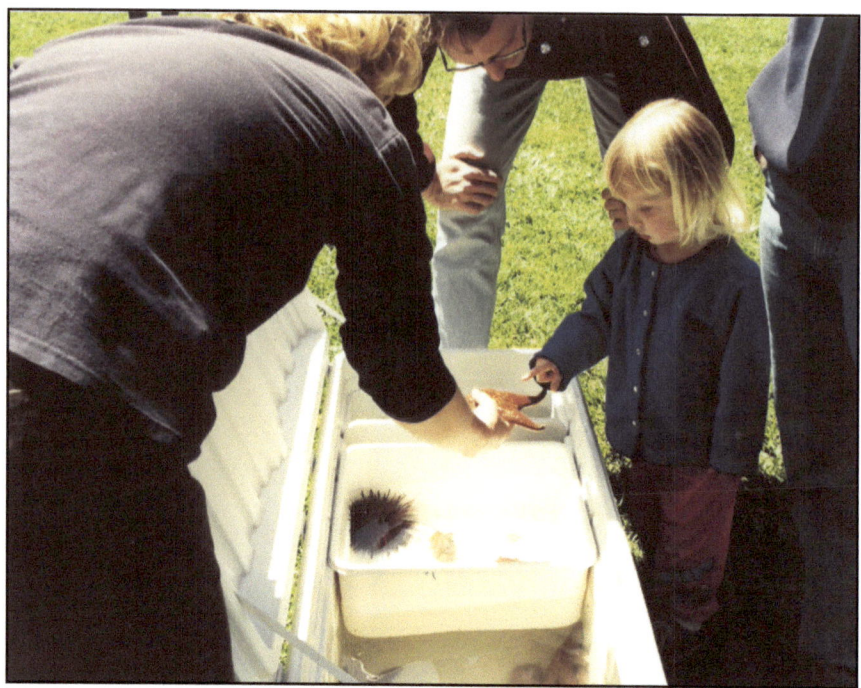

Kids Club allowed children to learn in new ways, often with hands on experience.

it to reflect on how the games physically illustrated the difference between what we termed the traditional educational paradigm and the Service Learning/Y.E.S. House paradigm. As leaders, valuing a shift in how we relate to one another, we challenged ourselves to intentionally and consciously step into this way of being together with each other, with our volunteers, and with folks we served."

> "Y.E.S. House was such an important part of my college years. It allowed me the opportunity to get involved in the community. I met so many great friends and people through Y.E.S. House. I also learned valuable skills about being a leader, fundraising, interviewing to name just a few. Whenever I see Y.E.S. House posts on Facebook I feel a sadness that I'm no longer part of that community but an excitement for all the students who have also found a special place there!"

-Stephanie Matkins,
Hand-In-Hand Co-Director &
Program Consultant

Y.E.S.

Y.E.S. received support when Governor Gray Davis and the legislature gave the California State University system $2.2 million to implement or expand service learning in 2000. Becoming the largest higher education institution to offer those programs, the CSU committed to matching the state funds with at least $2 million from other sources. Since then, the CSU's Call to Service Initiative has received more than $20 million to help develop

Camping trips were a great way for participants to experience nature.

2000s

This flyer encouraged volunteering with the program.

new service-learning courses or expand service-learning offices on all 23 CSU campuses.

In 2009, the Chancellor's Office recognized Y.E.S. as one of four exemplary service learning organizations in the California State University system in a student leadership manual called *Advancing Community Engagement with Student Leaders: A 'How-To' Manual from the California State University*. "HSU and Y.E.S. were seen as leaders specifically around student leadership," Bolick-Floss says. Using Humboldt State as a template, the manual highlighted

Y.E.S.

Retreat was a memorable experience for many Y.E.S. volunteers

how the involvement of student leaders in community engagement efforts promoted improvements in programming strategies, campus-community partnerships, and building bridges between academic affairs and student affairs. For the students involved, programs like Y.E.S. gave them practical experience and skills, exposure to career opportunities, self-confidence and self-worth, and opportunities to make deeper connections with peers and the community, along with campus leaders, faculty, and staff.

"Oh my gosh, lots of great memories! The training retreats are probably my favorite. Between each semester, we usually would have a three-day overnight training and we always had a service project so it brought people together in service… [T]hose retreats I think were really essential in terms of bonding and for [the students] to recognize they were also each other's support systems."

-Annie Bolick-Floss, Y.E.S. Executive Director/ Service Learning Coordinator (1994–2013)

Student leader retreats provide critical training for directors, as well as bonding and new experiences in nature.

By 2008, Y.E.S. had 40 years of experience in supporting student success, community engagement, and the community itself. The recognition and appreciation of Y.E.S. that had emerged on campus in the 1980s had now reached statewide proportions. But Y.E.S. has never been one to rest on its success. The 2010s would see continued innovation and programming to meet the expressed needs of the community.

2000s

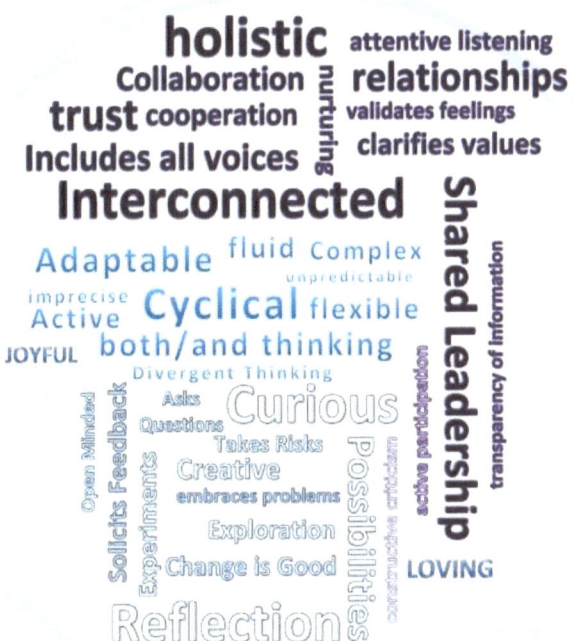

> **This visual demonstrates Y.E.S. values and reminds us to reflect on shifting paradigms.**
>
> -Lorena Boswell, Y.E.S. Program Manager and Coordinator (2008–2016)

Y.E.S.

The Motivational "Bathroom Poem"

This poem was painted on the wall of the Y.E.S. House bathroom in the late 2000s by Lorena Boswell. It has been an inspiration to many volunteers throughout the years. The original author is unknown.

**If there ever was a time to dare,
to make a differrence,
to embark on something worth doing,
it is now.**

**Not for any grand cause necessarily —
but for something that tugs at your heart,
something that's your aspiration,
something that's your dream.
You owe it to yourself tomake the days here count.**

**There will be good days,
and there will be bad days.
There will be times
when you want to turn around,
pack it up and call it quits.
Those times tell you that you are pushing yourself,
that you are not afraid to learn by trying.
Persist.**

Because with the right ideas, determination,
and the right tools
you can do great things.
Let your instincts, your intellect
and your heart guide you.
Trust.

Believe in the incredible power
of the human mind.
Have fun. Dig Deep. Stretch.
Dream Big.

Know, though, that things worth doing
seldom come easy.
Of doing something that makes
a difference, of working hard, of laughing
and hoping, of lazy afternoons,
of lasting friends, of all the
things that will cross your path this year.
The start of something new
brings the hope of something great.
Anything is possible.
There is only one you
And you will pass this way only once.
Do it right.

> "I've gained so much at Y.E.S. I don't even know how to quantify it. There's a sense of home when you come to the Y.E.S. House."

—Sam Nickles,
QMAP Director and
Program Consultant (2017–2019)

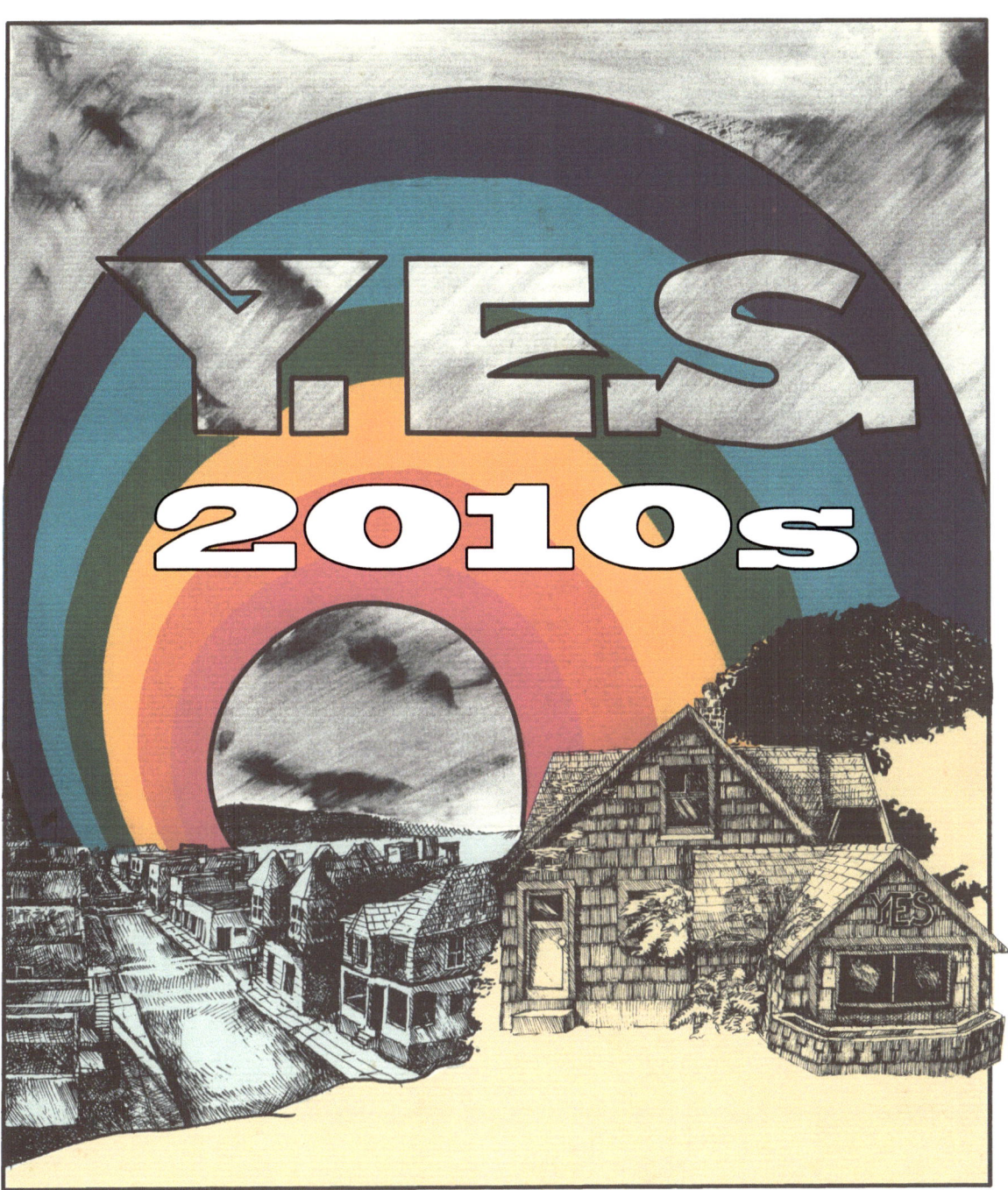

Y.E.S.

2010s

Fifty years of community collaboration is an extraordinary accomplishment. The successful community engagement and student leadership development owes much to the dedication and hardwork of students, their adaptation to meet the needs of the community, and community partners that opened the door to Y.E.S. volunteers.

Y.E.S. leaders and staff pose together during the Fall 2016 retreat at Blue Slide Camp in Maple Creek.

Student leaders work happily together during a Spring Retreat volunteer project at the Jefferson Community Center in Eureka (2017).

One notable highlight of the 2010s was the actualization of the first LGBTQIA+ program at Y.E.S. Founded by Diana Diyarza and Amanda Near in 2015, the Queer Mentoring and Advocacy Program (QMAP) provided mentoring and advocacy for LBGTQIA+ youth in local high schools. Program volunteers visit schools where the volunteers share their knowledge of queer events and resources with the community at large. In the spirit of program adaptation, Director Jake Hanten noted the increasing difficulty in recruiting students to Tutorial, and so championed to change the Tutorial name to Study Buddies. The more friendly sounding name led to an immediate rise in interest in the program.

2010s

J.D., a relic from the early days of LEAP and now the unofficial mascot at Y.E.S., looks on as volunteers knit hats for older adults, oncology patients, and children in the community.

Y.E.S.

Traditionally a one-on-one program, Diana Diyarza introduced group service to Study Buddies, increasing its impact and appeal to volunteers.

During the 50 years of collaboration, Y.E.S. developed many long-lasting community partnerships, such as with Potawot Community Food Garden, the Jefferson Community Center, and local elementary and high schools. Alyse Eckenrode, Associate Principal at Pacific

Serve-a-Thon, held on Cesar Chavez Day, is the annual spring fundraiser and center-wide volunteer event at Y.E.S. Over 100 HSU students participate.

Union Elementary School, noted how valuable the volunteers from Study Buddies, Puentes, and Youth Mentoring have been working in small groups or one-on-one to provide extra support, mentoring, and guidance to students. Heidi Benzonelli, President of the Board of

Y.E.S.

Volunteers contribute over 350 collective hours to community projects during Serve-a-Thon.

Directors for Westside Community Improvement Association (WCIA), credited Y.E.S. with supporting the Jefferson Community Center's goals of sustainability and social responsibility and how "we are where we are because of the participation of Humboldt State students."

> "The volunteers themselves are a little family and there for each other. It's a very supportive kind of space. That's how it was when we directed QMAP. We found that it wasn't only providing support for the queer youth community, but it was a support group for all of us… [QMAP] was the best thing I've ever done with my life."
>
> -Amanda Near,
> YMP Director, QMAP Co-Founder and Director (2013–2016)

Y.E.S.

Elizabeth Deck, Y.E.S. Office Manager, works in the kitchen during a Director's Retreat.

Since the beginning, Y.E.S. has helped volunteers develop leadership experience, professional skills, and personal growth and transformation. Marilyn Liu, a Y.E.S. alumnus and recipient of the Al Elpusan Award for Student Activism at HSU in Spring 2016, directed the

STEP UPP volunteers prepare food at Project Open Hand, an organization providing nutritious meals to seniors and critically ill neighbors in San Francisco (Alternative Spring Break (2018).

ART program from 2013–2014. Liu reported how her experiences at Y.E.S. was an integral factor in her success beyond HSU and allowed her to believe in her "power to foster transformations within the people I lead." She continued that "Y.E.S. ingrained my personal mantra to consistently keep the community I work with, and the big picture, in mind, no matter where I am." The thousands of Y.E.S. volunteers echo that spirit, carrying the spirit of Y.E.S. within themselves and sharing it with the world the rest of their lives.

Y.E.S.

Y.E.S. leaders geared up to kayak on the bay for a retreat team-building adventure led by Center Activities.

> " **A lot of the kids who are in most need of support or attention don't have the resources to get a one-on-one person who is specifically looking out for them. Through the Y.E.S. program we've been able to provide those students with a person who focuses on just them, who makes them feel special, who helps them succeed.** "
>
> -Alyse Eckenrode, Associate Principal, Pacific Union School

2010s

Hand-In-Hand hosts a program fundraiser, selling DIY tie-dye shirts on the HSU Quad.

Y.E.S.

Kelly Fortner and Belen Gutierrez-Flores assist with recruitment efforts during the Y.E.S. Tabling Fair in the HSU Library lobby (Spring 2018).

> "Whenever anyone asks me about my college experience, Youth Educational Services is the first thing I tell them about. Through Y.E.S. I realized what career path I wanted to follow once I finished school, and gave me the tools necessary to achieve my dreams. But not only did it give me a career, Y.E.S. gave me a strong and loving community as well as a family. Some of the strongest friendships in my life exist because Y.E.S. introduced me to so many wonderful people. I'm so incredibly proud to have been part of Y.E.S."

-Tamara Valadez,
YMP Director
and Program Consultant
(2014-3017)

> "Y.E.S. has really changed my life in little ways and in major ways. I have focused my career goals and made wonderful relationships. I have learned about myself and my ability to work with kids, my peers, and community contacts. Y.E.S. is a wonderful place, I can't imagine my life without it and I will miss it very much."
>
> —Nichole Hillyer, Hand-In-Hand and Program Consultant

Y.E.S.

Beyond

As we begin our sixth decade, Youth Educational Services (Y.E.S.) continues to be a dynamic program for student development, self-discovery, career exploration, and community building. The reciprocal nature of campus and community partnerships has deepened the hands-on learning and impact of Y.E.S. programs. Over the past 50 years, more than 70 programs have been developed and sustained by student time, talent, and tenacity. These programs have been focused on local community needs and flavored by the social and political tides of each era.

Melea Smith (right) with Elizabeth Deck.

The Y.E.S. commitment to student leadership, community building, and social justice is as relevant now as it was in the 1960s. In the face of current social, environmental, and political issues, students at Y.E.S. continue to engage and work towards positive change. They harness and inspire hope and diversity through relationship building. Y.E.S. partnerships help cultivate bridges between campus and local communities. Through the years, over 5,000 volunteers and thousands of community members have benefited from Y.E.S. programs. That is an extraordinary impact for a predominantly rural community. These collaborations are not without challenges; volunteers must navigate real-world situations as an integral part of their community engagement experience and student leadership development. Y.E.S. students continue to initiate ideas and programs to meet shared needs, and to inspire each generation.

While working with HSU students during the past two years and after listening to the interviews conducted for this project, I am moved by what has remained constant at Y.E.S. over the years. Current and former community members bring to light the traditions that resonate over decades. These memories include Y.E.S potlucks, student leader retreats, games, and team building activities. Students truly gain a sense of belonging and home at Y.E.S. Many forge lasting friendships; a few even married their Y.E.S. sweetheart.

Volunteers and leaders also reflect that they gained as much or more from their experience than they contributed through their Y.E.S. program. Connecting with community members made a lasting impact on volunteers. They fondly remember moments shared with program participants, whether it be a homework lesson tackled, or the Humboldt wilderness explored on foot, horseback, or whitewater raft. These are the threads that weave together the contributions of five decades of Y.E.S. community members, a quilt created by hands and hearts of all ages.

In line with the Y.E.S. mission, this book was created by a team of remarkable students. Three Library Scholar Interns worked alongside HSU Library and Y.E.S. staff to capture the stories and memories of students and alumni. We hope this project stimulates further interest and helps build upon existing Y.E.S. connections and community development. There are countless student leaders, volunteers, former staff, campus and community partners, and program participants who have contributed to Y.E.S. We honor all the voices and perspectives shared, and those yet to be shared, that together form the powerful legacy of Y.E.S.

– Melea Smith, Y.E.S. Coordinator

Y.E.S Programs

Study Buddies (formerly Tutorial) 1968-present
YMP (formerly Big Brother –Friends Together) 1969-present
Spectrum West 1969-1970
Film Forum 1969-1970
Adult Aid 1969-1970
Consumer Services 1969-1970
Helping Hands 1969-1970
Education Support Services 1969-1972
Project Small Kid 1969-1971
Manila Recreation 1971-1973
Housing Project Recreation Program 1971-1973
Project Respond 1971-1975
Recycling 1971-1974
Neighborhood Center Day Camp 1972-1973
Contact 1972-1975
Adopt a Grandparent 1973-1990
Nutrition for Kids 1973-1990
Hand-in-Hand (formerly Day Camp, 5H, 4H) 1973-present
Stewart School Project 1974-1975
Health Education Rap Team 1974-1980
Car Pool 1974-1977
Juvenile Hall Recreation-Program 1974-1980. 2001-present
Legal Information & Referral 1974-1980
Learning Action Change 1975-1976
Innovations 1975-1977
Cinema YES 1976-1977
Consumer Information Advocate 1975-1978
Experimental College 1976-1977
MONEY 1967-1979
Friends 1976-1983
Connections 1976-1986
Horizons Unlimited 1976-1988
Environmental Education 1976-present
Indeed 1977-1983

Wertman the Wizard   1977-1978
Welfare Outreach   1977-1978
Children's Community Garden Project   1977-1978
Volunteer in Tax Assistance   1977-1979
Greenpeace Sea Watch   1978-1984
Together in Sign   1978-1980
Cultural Exchange   1978-1985
YES Travel   1978-1980
C.C.A.T. (Campus Center for Approp. Tech)   1978-1981
LEAP   1979-present
Draft Information – Think First   1979-1989
Kids Club of Manila   1980-1982
Family Focus – SNAP   1983-2001
4-H Trail / T.R.U.S.T.   1985-1989
Teen Theater   1985-1989
Southeast Asian Outreach Program   1986-2006
Special Projects – Into the Streets   1987-1990
Escort Service – Students for Safe Community   1988-1989
Global Education – Club Oppression   1990-1993
Community Companions Adults – Mental Health Education   1990-2007

Community Companions Youth   1990-2004
Sign in School   1991-1992
New Games   1991-present
No Means No   1991-1993
Peer Counseling   1992-1993
Homelessness Network   1993-present
Puentes   1994-presnt
Cultural Ties – Youth Solutions   1994-1997
STAR (Students Talking About Race)   1995-1998
Humboldt Community Service International   1997-2002
Sustainable Campus Task Force   1999-2000
North Coast Music Mentors   2003-present
Volunteer Opportunity Program (VOP)   2006-present
ASB (STEP UPP)   1995-present
ART Recreation Theater   2006-present
BEST (on hold as of S17)   2014-present
QMAP (final semester of pilot status)

*Please note there may be discrepancies between program dates listed here and in the text due to the varying source materials.

Acknowledgments

Thank you to the great team that made this book possible.

Library Scholar Internship Team:
Amanda Ramirez-Sebree, research, layout
Erika Andrews, author
Stan Smith, videographer

Managing team:
Elizabeth Deck, Y.E.S. Office Manager
Carly Marino, Special Collections Librarian
Kyle Morgan, Scholarly Communications & Digital Scholarship Librarian
Cyril Oberlander, Dean of the University Library
Melea Smith, Y.E.S. Coordinator
Tay D. Triggs, Director of Office of Student Life

Student staff team:
Sarah Godlin, Editorial, Layout, and Design
Emma Hanley, Research
Carolyn Delevich, Editorial
Amanda Alster, Layout Assistance

Interviewees:

Heidi Benzonelli, President of Westside Community Improvement Association
Annie Bolick Floss, Y.E.S. Executive Director/Service Learning Coordinator
(1994–2013)
Diana Diyarza Study Buddies Director, Program Consultant,
QMAP Co-Founder and Director (2012–2016)
Alyse Eckenrode, Associate Principal, Pacific Union School
Ben Fairless, Y.E.S. Director and Professor of Social Work (1968–2001)
Amanda Near, YMP Director, QMAP Co-Founder and Director (2013–2016)
Fernando Paz, Y.E.S. Puentes Volunteer (2005), CCAE Coordinator (2018)
Amanda Ramirez-Sebree, Y.E.S. Volunteer and Leader (2014–2018)
Jim Ritter, Y.E.S. Volunteer and Leader (1979–1984)
Ray Watson, Facility Manager, Humboldt County Juvenile Hall
Mark Weller, Deputy Director, Westside Community Improvement Association
John Woolley, Y.E.S. Co-Founder and Leader (1967–1972)

Additional support and reviews provided by:

Humboldt State University Marketing and Communications
Keaundrey Clark, Videographer
Cheryl Conner, Editorial
Kellie Jo Brown, Photographer

Special thanks to:

Humboldt State University
California State University

How You Can Help

As we celebrate 50 years of community building, we invite you to honor and promote the mission and achievements of Y.E.S. We encourage you to write us about how Y.E.S. impacted you or to share your favorite memory. We also encourage your support of Y.E.S. Donations will help future student leaders and support community engagement locally and beyond HSU. Your investment in Y.E.S. has a long-lasting impact on the lives of students and the community. Donations are needed to support volunteer training and screening and for the variety of programs that require travel to various communities.

Please visit **alumni.humboldt.edu/giving/yes** or contact us for more details. There are opportunities to endow support to your favorite programs, or planned giving to ensure the next 50 years at Y.E.S. is even more vibrant and impactful. We greatly appreciate the support of Y.E.S. volunteers and donors, and as this history has shown, what a positive difference we are making in this world.

This book was made possible with the help of the Library Scholar Internship Program at Humboldt State University.

This unique program allows Library Scholar Interns to benefit from project-based learning that produces high-impact online content. Library Scholar Interns work in collaboration with academic programs and each other to build skills in teamwork, problem solving, communications, and research. Library Scholar Interns lead projects such as researching and writing for the web, curating exhibits and engagement programs, creating presentations, and publishing and digitizating content. Interns are paid and may receive course credit. Interns also receive credit for their online productions. Interns also recieve public acknowledgement for their creative and scholarly works.

More information on individual internships and current position openings can be found by visiting:

http://library.humboldt.edu/about/internships

Intern Team

Stan Smith

Stan Smith recorded and edited the video interviews.

Stan was raised in Sacramento, California, and earned his associates degree in film and media studies from Cosumnes River College before transferring to the Humboldt State University film department. An avid outdoorsman and geography minor, Stan enjoys taking advantage of the numerous hiking trails, beautiful beaches, and walkability of Arcata before inevitably heading down to Southern California to pursue a career in the film industry.

"Working as an intern with Y.E.S. and the library staff was a pleasure! The ability to film such interesting and upstanding former volunteers and collaborators gave me an insight into the history and value of youth services and volunteering that I would have never had the privilege of experiencing otherwise. I am happy to have worked with such pleasant and respectful colleagues, and was always treated well throughout the summer by Melea and Kyle. Anyone who has the chance to work as an intern with Y.E.S. should never pass up such an opportunity!"

Erika Andrews

Erika Andrews wrote the body text.

Erika is currently a senior at Humboldt State University, majoring in English: Writing Practices with a minor in Comparative Ethnic Studies. This is her first publication. She is the 2018–19 Member at Large for the Epsilon Upsilon Chapter of Delta Phi Epsilon Sorority Inc., as well as the Assistant Managing Editor for the *Toyon: Multilingual Journal of Literature and Art*. Erika is an inspiring poet and filmmaker. Erika hails from Paramount, California, and hopes that she is making little girls who look like her proud.

"When I think of my internship with Humboldt Scholars, Special Collection, and the Y.E.S. House, I am truly amazed at what we were able to produce in such little time. While writing about the Y.E.S. House, every decade I researched, I became more intrigued and inspired. The commitment Y.E.S. has to the community is humbling. From radical student organization to long-standing community collaborator, Y.E.S. has never lost sight of their vision of community participation.

I urge those that have a heart for volunteering, an investment in the betterment of the Humboldt community, and those seeking to find a family within the Redwood Curtain, to seek out Y.E.S. or support them in any way possible. I may not have been a volunteer of Y.E.S. before writing this book but I am grateful that I could gift them a small token of my gratitude for all they have done and all that is yet to do.

I do not know where this opportunity will take me in the future but I sure am honored that I get to find out. I would like to congratulate Y.E.S. for 50 beautiful years of community building, the wonderful library staff who stood beside me through this journey, and to the communities that keep organizations like Y.E.S. going, this is for you."

Sarah Godlin

Sarah Godlin typeset and designed this book.

    Sarah is a writer and book designer who works as a student intern in the Humboldt State University Library in Publishing and Special Collections. She is the Production Editor of *Toyon: Multilingual Journal of Literature and Art*, and has designed four books and written one. You can find more of her design work at greengolde.com

Amanda Ramirez-Sebree

Amanda Ramirez-Sebree was the lead researcher on this project. She facilitated the interviews and provided the framework for the book.

    Amanda is an Environmental Science & Management: Planning & Policy major. She is originally from San Bernardino, CA. See the Preface on page ix for more information on Amanda and her internship experience.

www.ingramcontent.com/pod-product-compliance
Lightning Source LLC
Chambersburg PA
CBHW050753110526
44592CB00003B/55